GOD'S HEART FOR HIS PEOPLE IN AMERICA
AS WE FACE UNCERTAIN TIMES...

IF MY PEOPLE

IN CASE OF
NATIONAL EMERGENCY
READ THIS

SHANE IDLEMAN

Published by El Paseo Publications
PO Box 3486
Lancaster, Ca. 93586

Printed in the United States of America

ISBN: 978-1-7343774-1-5

Contents

Important Note from the Author

Although I recommend articles and authors in this book, I do not endorse them or always agree with their position. My goal is to offer the reader as much information as possible.

If you're reading the print version of this book, my encouragement is to also download the e-book version as well so that you can read the articles and listen to the sermons that are mentioned throughout this book. My books are all available at ShaneIdleman.com.

A special thank you to Christine Ramsey as well as Liz Smith for jumping right on this project and offering a second set of eyes on editing and structure.

Introduction

The Destabilization of America

It seems that everyone is sensing the destabilization of America. Books could be written on how we got to this point, but let me offer just a few thoughts from a biblical perspective.[1]

Destabilization by false information. Unless you have been on Mars or had your head in the sand for the last decade, you have clearly seen how so many in the secular media purposely create false narratives and use lies and carefully edited half-truths to push their agenda. They withhold information, such as reporting on the number of black police officers who have been killed recently, and deliberately fail to highlight the positives alongside the negatives, creating the illusion of an imbalance where one does not exist. For example, two years ago a deputy sheriff who attends our church had to pull over on the freeway to resuscitate a black female suffering from a drug overdose. I tried to contact several news outlets, but no one wanted to run the story.

The lesson here is to be cautious about where we get our information. Much of the media is owned by large corporations who would love to see America fail. One recent headline read, "CNN sticks to liberal script, ignores black police officers killed in riots."[2] This is appalling and should not be tolerated.

Destabilization by the enemy within. Many people are coming to believe that what we are witnessing is an orchestrated attempt to destroy our economy and disrupt elections. Peaceful protests are infiltrated by hate groups paid by individuals with deep pockets to create confusion and chaos. Why is there such a huge upheaval? It's simple: The current administration has become a major roadblock to the liberal agenda. They are working to minimize the murdering of babies via abortion, and they are actively addressing racial and socioeconomic issues and trying to do the right thing the right way. They are being a terror to terrorists and are bringing the Bible and God back to Washington and the nation's schools. They want to remove the pulpit-silencing Johnson Amendment. Christians with godly values are being promoted to some of the highest offices in America. The president is surrounding himself with godly counsel. There is a love for Israel. They are honoring hard work and minimizing free handouts. The list of Christ-honoring accomplishments is impressive. Now you see what the real battle is: *A battle for the soul of our nation.* God doesn't judge a nation based on the character of one man; He judges it based on the spiritual health of its people. Never forget that.

Destabilization by intolerability. Those waving banners of tolerance are often the most intolerant toward those who oppose them, as one Birmingham pastor recently discovered. Tony Perkins writes, "A handful of *likes* were all it took to make the biggest church in Alabama homeless." Believe it or not, "a local English teacher decided to catalogue" the pastor's likes on Facebook and then share them with the press.[3] This motivated the local high schools to revoke the church's lease. Am I the only one who sees the hypocrisy of school district "leaders" and teachers who behave in this manner while crying out for tolerance and justice?

Destabilization with class warfare. Rasmussen recently reported that there is a 40 percent approval rate for our president among black voters, but if you listen to the secular media, you would think that it's closer to 4 percent. Yes, there is racism in America, and not just among whites, but only a changed heart can solve that. And keep in mind that this has been a long time in the making. Revisionists began to rewrite history many years ago, portraying all white people as racists. The actual numbers are trivial; the vast majority are not racists. And there are black racists and white racists and racists of every shade in between too. We need to realize that we are all Americans and must unite against our common enemy. It's a sin problem, not a skin problem. White people also feel the dynamic. I can no longer go to certain places in my community, such as parks, for fear of being profiled, because the media has created a false narrative. You won't find it in many of the modern history books, but the truth is that many of the Founding Fathers in America abhorred slavery and fought against it.[4]

Destabilization fueled by the passive pulpit. I recently saw a survey on Facebook that asked, "Do you feel that most church leaders speak up about the real issues facing us today?" The overwhelming response was a very loud and clear no. Christians are looking to pastors to lead the way, but many are exchanging truth for tolerance, boldness for "balance," and conviction for cowardliness. They don't want to offend for fear they might lose their audience. Pastors and Christian leaders alike must take responsibility for the spiritual health of our nation—and whether we accept that responsibility or not, God Himself will hold us accountable. The pulpit inevitably sets the tone of the religious climate of the nation. A culture devoid of God simply reflects the lack of conviction in the pulpit as well as the pew. The silent pulpit is not God's pulpit.

Destabilization because kingdoms are colliding. I believe that the next hammer to fall will be a spike in COVID-19—that is, if the riots don't accomplish their intended purpose first. There is also a great deal going on behind the scenes with generals and other elected and unelected officials divided against President Trump. The real reason, in many cases, is because many of these people are holdovers from the last administration (what is commonly referred to as the Deep State). So, of course they are upset and seeking to be divisive; it is a strategic play designed to protect themselves. Subpoenas are being served, crimes are being investigated, and perversion is being exposed, bringing huge upheaval. Kingdoms are colliding. All this is a clear demonstration of Romans 1. People are rejecting God, and He is giving them over to a debased and corrupted mind. How else can they justify killing children while promoting deviant sexual behavior? There is no fear of God in the land.

How sad that many churches won't even do voter registration because it's "too political." God ordained the government; surely He doesn't want us to stay silent. What we say (or do not say) greatly impacts politics. We are not being political; we are being biblical. Saying, "I'm just not political," is really an excuse to hide cowardliness. My friend and fellow pastor Jim Garlow commented, "Bold pastors may look like they are on the wrong side of history, but they are on the right side of eternity."

Many are even marching with ungodly groups and seeking redemption by kneeling. This is why the social gospel is so dangerous—it removes redemption through Christ and places it on "good works," making it no gospel at all. There is no harm in calling out national sins; we have biblical grounds for that, as we see in the life of Daniel and Nehemiah. But is racism the only sin we are guilty of as a nation? Why not unite black and white pastors in peaceful, biblically-grounded, gospel-centered,

God-honoring gatherings rather than align with groups who fuel anger, revel in sin, and take pride in the lack of forgiveness and unity in their mission statements?[5]

Patience Is Not Approval

What's happening in America is called *psychological warfare*, and it may get worse before it gets better. The goal of some is to elevate stress to the point of exhaustion (e.g., stay-at-home orders) and then fuel fear so that people give up their rights (e.g., mandatory mask-wearing, riots). To win the psychological battle (the battle of the mind), one must saturate their mind in the Word and ways of God. We need to look up at God and not look around at what is going on. Churches need prayer meetings and worship nights, even if it's just a small group of people. God doesn't look for huge crowds; He looks for broken hearts. America's heart needs to break so that deep repentance takes place.

Do we really think that we can flood our homes with porn, murder millions of children, satiate the gods of alcohol, lust, and addiction, mock God's Word, declare war on the family, excuse racism, promote self-centered politicians, and idolize celebrity pastors who tip-toe around sin, and expect a wonderful life for our nation? No, we cannot. What also is coming down is an ungodly foundation. Isaiah 30:1 (NASB) sheds much-needed light on what is happening: "'Woe to the rebellious children,' declares the LORD, 'who execute a plan, but not Mine, and make an alliance, but not of My Spirit, in order to add sin to sin.'"

As in the prophet Joel's day, today "joy has withered away from the sons of men" (Joel 1:12 NKJV). Instead of complaining, we need to obey God, who says, "Consecrate a fast, call a sacred assembly; gather the elders and all the inhabitants of the land into the house of the LORD your God, and cry out to the LORD" (v. 14 NKJV). In a sense, God is saying, "How bad do you want deliverance? Will you turn to Me with all your heart? Will you starve the flesh to be filled with the Spirit via prayer and fasting? Will you humble yourself and repent?"

That's what this book is about, because if we do, we are reminded that God is merciful and slow to anger. But we must stop confusing His patience with His approval.

Revival is not just an emotional touch; it's a complete takeover!

– Nancy Leigh Demoss

Humility

The First Step
Toward Revival

> If My people who are called by My name
> will humble themselves, and pray and seek
> My face, and turn from their wicked ways,
> then I will hear from heaven, and will
> forgive their sin and heal their land.
> — 2 Chronicles 7:14

I recently had the privilege of speaking[6] to our church audience about revival, with 2 Chronicles 7:14 as the backdrop. The sacred text says, "If my people, which are called by my name, shall humble themselves, and pray, and seek my face, and turn from their wicked ways; then will I hear from heaven, and will forgive their sin, and will heal their land." Note that it does not say, "If Hollywood or Washington or the media turns to God" but "if My people" turn.

It's no surprise that we are witnessing the rapid deterioration of a nation right before our eyes. As a result, many are struggling with fear and anxiety and uncertainty, yet God offers hope—tremendous hope.

I can already hear the critics: "Second Chronicles 7:14 does not apply to us. It was for Israel." As one who understands the importance of theology in its context, I can appreciate this statement. Many Scriptures, when taken out of context, have done great damage to the church and our witness. The context of 2 Chronicles is that when God brings judgment on His people as a result of their sins, He will heal their land (think rain and a bountiful harvest). God said if they humble themselves, pray, seek Him, and turn from their sin, that He would re-establish His blessings.

For those who don't like using this verse in modern America, consider these questions: Is it a bad thing if America humbles itself, prays, seeks God, and repents? Is it possible that blessings could follow such an outpour of repentance and spiritual renewal? Absolutely! Although the direct *context* may not apply to us, the *principle* always applies. There are crucial principles throughout the Old Testament, principles that can lead to national restoration amid catastrophes. Our nation's current spiritual climate motivated me to write this book. Although many have written exceptional books on revival, prayer, and fasting, I felt God leading me to release something more current.

With that said, let's take a look at the first principle found in 2 Chronicles 7:14—*humility.*

During the COVID-19 Safer-at-Home order, God poured His Spirit powerfully into my heart even though I was preaching to a camera. Throughout seasons like that of the coronavirus and the civil unrest and protests that have followed, we must realize that revival is our only hope. During one sermon, I looked at a key statement found in Isaiah 58. God told His people that He was done with phony sacrifices and hard-hearted obedience. He said that things had to change if they wanted "to make [their] voice heard on high" (v. 4). And just like the Israelites back then, things need to change in America if we want God to truly hear our prayers. While we have been too full of pride, complacency, and apathy to experience revival, the current national crisis can be a catalyst.

Revival is not about scheduling a series of meetings, nor is it acting weird and loud. Revival can't be worked up; it must be brought down. Winkie Pratney said, "Revival brings back a holy shock to apathy and carelessness." Revival is when God's power meets God's people—when we experience the fire of God and are forever changed. God's fire burns but does not consume; it refines but does not destroy. It's been said that God is a consuming fire, the Holy Spirit brings the fire, John the

Baptist preached fire, and Jesus said that we would receive fire. *Revival fire* is the urgent need today.

Dead in the Church of the Living God

Although revival can't be generated in and of ourselves, it can be fueled as men and women seek the heart of God personally and corporately through repentance, worship, fellowship, and prayer. Leonard Ravenhill, in his compelling book *Revival Praying,* wrote, "Since something is obviously stopping the Spirit's inflow to us Christians, the same thing is stopping His outflow from us. With the Spirit's help, we need to search for this hindrance."[7]

The "hindrance" is often pride and spiritual apathy. I believe that's why 2 Chronicles opens with humility; it truly is the first step. The greatest need in the lives of Christians today is to remove pride so that the power of the Holy Spirit can flow through us. Always remember that you are as revived as you want to be. But be warned, those on fire for God often convict those who are not. A mighty move of God's Spirit always creates friction in the church. Carnal Christians and modern-day Pharisees will disdain you because they lack intimacy with God. Their statements go something like this:

"Let's not get too carried away."

"You are too emotional."

"What's all this talk about revival?"

"God doesn't do that anymore."

Trust me, friends, God is not pleased with carnality or a church resembling a cemetery. Cemeteries may be calm and orderly, but there is no life there. How can we be dead spiritually in the church of the living God?

Granted, even though revival by its very nature produces emotional excitement, we must be careful. Iain H. Murray warns us to be open but cautious when it comes to emotions:

> The course of a revival, together with its purity and abiding fruit, is directly related to the manner in which such excitement is handled by its leaders. Once the idea gains acceptance that the degree of the Spirit's work is to be measured by the strength of emotion, or that physical effects of any kind are proof of God's action, then what is rightly called fanaticism is bound to follow. For those who embrace such beliefs will suppose that any check on the emotion or on physical phenomenon is tantamount to opposing the Holy Spirit.[8]

Some will be jealous when they see you experiencing God if they are not. They often fall under the hard-hearted church mentioned in Revelation 2:1–7. Hard hearts can easily point out false doctrine, work hard in ministry, and obey God in conspicuous areas, but God still calls them to repent for what lies beneath the surface: "But I have this against you, that you have left your first love" (v. 4 NASB). If they don't repent, God will judge them.

I often talk about when I was a modern-day Pharisee with a stony heart. I didn't care about love; I cared about being right. I would say that I was standing for the truth in order to cover my spiritual pride. Yes, the truth will offend others, but our attitude should not offend them. Pharisaical Christians have the truth, but they lack the fruit of the Spirit, such as joy, gentleness, and love. Spiritual pride is deadly.

Once I experienced a mighty move of God's Spirit in my heart (personal revival), I felt like the blind man who was grilled by the arrogant religious leaders. Today, their grilling would go something like this: "What exactly did Jesus do to you? We want a theological exposition of what happened and a biblically accurate, conservative, hermeneutic approach to the technique He used."

Like the blind man, I don't know exactly how God does it, but one thing I do know: I was blind, but now I see! I've tasted and seen the goodness of God. I didn't want God's presence, but today I'm a lover of His presence. I didn't like deep worship, but now it's the heartbeat of my soul. I plead with you: Don't be dead in the church of the living God.

Taking the First Step

As I stated earlier, you are as revived as you want to be. If this upsets you, simply repent of your calloused heart, and do not hide behind the excuse, "But I have the truth." So did the Pharisees, and we know how that turned out. Revival doesn't minimize the truth; it elevates it.

As I read *The Journals of George Whitefield* and the eyewitness accounts of the Welsh revivals and the First Great Awakening in America, I find that Jonathan Edwards's words ring true. He observed that a work of the Holy Spirit would be evident because it would: 1) elevate the truth, 2) exalt Christ, 3) oppose Satan, 4) point people to the Scriptures, and 5) result in love for God and others. The focus was on preaching the totality of God's Word, calling out sin, and correcting error. Holiness, not hysteria, is evident, and the result is genuine fruit, not ungodly fanaticism.

Do you lack this fire of God? What do you do when you're physically cold? You run to the fire, to the warmth. In the same way, when you're spiritually cold, you must run to the fire of God. You must have desperation and a deep desire to encounter His presence. Repentance is always the first step toward revival. Revival is a downpour, and repentance opens the floodgates.

Revival is like farming. The farmer can't make the seed grow, but he can create an environment for growth. We must be careful with absolute statements like "Fasting will always lead to revival" because it will not happen if our hearts are wrong. It may also be delayed according to God's sovereignty. We also can't always use 2 Chronicles 7:14 as a magic recipe we just have to carefully follow and God is somehow obligated to produce the desired result. However, any group of people who humbles themselves via fasting, prays fervently, seeks God, and turns from their sins will get the attention of God. If 2 Chronicles is not sufficient to encourage you in this, consider God's promise in Jeremiah when He says, "And you will seek Me and find Me, when you search for Me with all your heart" (Jeremiah 29:13). Our obedience, love, repentance, and passionate seeking of Christ can no doubt spark the flames of revival if God grants us that wonderful blessing.

The process of revival and hope must begin with humility. Andrew Murray said, "Pride must die in you, or nothing of heaven can live in you." The amount of pride in the church is astonishing. We've created an *American Idol* mentality, with many wanting center-stage attention. We often look more like Hollywood than the character of Christ. James 4:6 says that "God resists the proud, but gives grace to the humble." If you are being humbled, don't fight it! God disciplines those He loves.

If we are to see a genuine move of God—which is the only hope for our nation—then we must humble ourselves and confess our pride. Our blessings have become a curse; our abundance has taken us away from God. Pride is so powerful that many people reading this will get upset rather than humble themselves and seek God afresh. I have not mastered this area. I'm a prideful person working on humility daily. But we must recognize our own pride, repent of it, and return to God with a broken and teachable attitude.

Revival is when God gets so sick and tired of being misrepresented that He shows up Himself.

– Leonard Ravenhill

Prayer

The Sin of
Prayerlessness

I must have looked like a deer caught in the headlights when I heard the words: "Why are we having another prayer and worship night?" A few years ago, we offered a night of prayer and worship each month, but apparently, that was too much for a few individuals, and they made sure to let me know.

I enjoy preaching and listening to sermons. But Jesus said, "My house shall be called a house of prayer," and 2 Chronicles 7:14 says, "If My people . . . pray." Prayer is the life source to our faith, the building block of our soul. God is not too busy; He's not on vacation; He's not sleeping. He is an ever-present help in times of need. You can call on Him at two in the morning or in the midst of the storm. He hears the prayers of His children, but five-minute devotions aren't going to cut it in these dire times. We must cultivate a life of prayer fueled by brokenness and humility so that we become men and women clothed with power from on high. Those who do the most for God are always people of prayer.

Sadly, the sin of prayerlessness is running rampant in many of our churches. The dry, dead lethargic condition of the church clearly reflects an impotent prayer life. Prayerlessness in the pulpit leads to apostasy and dead sermons. Prayerlessness in the pew leads to shattered lives and depression. Prayerlessness in men leads to the breakdown of the family. Prayerlessness in Washington leads to the breakdown of society. As E. M. Bounds stated, "When faith ceases to pray, it ceases to live."

When the Church Had Power

Is America's future hopeless? The Bible is clear that God judges wickedness and reprimands His people. Many of the Old Testament prophets experienced hardship and exile as the result of God reprimanding His people. In short, He reprimands to spark repentance, and He judges the wicked because they don't repent from their sin. Many are divided because although we realize America is ripe for judgment for atrocities ranging from aborting babies to redefining truth, we also see countless Christians seeking God with all their heart. Many examples can be found in the Old Testament of God staying His hand of judgment when righteous people contend and plead for revival and mercy. That's my hope for America.

God doesn't want us to sit back, relax, and wait for Jesus's return. We must expose the unfruitful works of darkness and fight demonic oppression, but to do that, we need spiritual power. Duncan Campbell, in his book *The Price and Power of Revival* makes a compelling point: "How is it that while we make such great claims for the power of the Gospel, we see so little of the supernatural in operation? Is there any reason why the Church today cannot everywhere equal the Church at Pentecost?"[9] No, there is no reason why. We are as revived as we want to be.

We believe in the fullness and the power of the Spirit, but few truly experience it. Most of the church needs to be revived, beginning with prayer. But corporate and national revival begins as individual men and women humbly and brokenly seek the heart of God through prayer and fasting. Here is just one example of a powerful move of God from Duncan Campbell:

> I think again of those people in the Hebrides. How they longed and how they prayed and how they waited and how they cried, "Oh God, rend the heavens and come down," and all the time God was handling them; all the time God was dealing with them and the process of cleansing went on until the moment came when angels and

archangels looking over the battlements of glory, cried, "God, the vessels are clean, the miracle can happen now." I believe that with all my heart — it is the deep conviction of my soul — that they are ever gazing over the battlements of glory and waiting for a prepared people."[10]

News headlines often read, "Churches are closing, and Christianity is on the decline." The truth is that Jesus's church is stronger than ever throughout the world. He is building His church, and the gates of hell cannot prevail (Matthew 16:18). But it does beg the question: Why does the church as a whole appear so impotent?

Leonard Ravenhill's powerful quote is worth repeating. "Since something is obviously stopping the Spirit's inflow to us Christians, the same thing is stopping His outflow from us. With the Spirit's help, we need to search for this hindrance." Notice he does not say "With the law's help..." The letter of the law kills, but the Spirit gives life! (See 2 Corinthians 3:6.) The law can lead to pride, and we have covered how that can block the channels of God's blessing in our lives—because God will not share His glory with another, even people as worthy as ourselves (that is a sarcastic statement, in case that is not clear—there is only One worthy).

Proud people lack humility and passionate prayer, for it's hard to desire something you don't think you need. They have the letter of the law but not the heart of Christ; good theology, but hard hearts. Sadly, those in this camp don't think that revival is biblical. They are proud, unteachable, and eager to dispute. Like the church in Ephesus, they must see their need. Jesus said, "I hold this against you: You have forsaken the love you had at first. Consider how far you have fallen! Repent and do the things you did at first" (Revelation 2:4-5 NIV).

The lukewarm church, on the other hand, disdains the heat of conviction; thus, it remains lukewarm. When I consider the lukewarm church, I'm often reminded of a book by Wilbur Rees, in which he stated, "I would like to buy $3 worth of God, please. Not enough to explode my soul or disturb my sleep, but just enough to equal a cup of warm milk or a snooze in the sunshine." Rees continues, "I want ecstasy, not transformation. I want the warmth of the womb, not a new birth. I want a pound of the Eternal in a paper sack. I would like to buy $3 worth of God, please."[11] This is indeed sad but very characteristic of many today.

Both groups, the proud and the lukewarm, must come to full repentance and total abandonment of their former ways. The Holy Spirit, always watching for a believer's deep repentance, moves quickly to restore and rebuild that person's life. As a result, he or she will develop a passion for prayer, a humble spirit, and a desire to share the grace and kindness of the Lord with others through their words and their good works.

Sustaining the Flame

Repentance clearly sparks the flame of revival and spiritual renewal, but prayer and fasting fuel the fire. What starts revival also maintains revival. Don't let familiar words like *prayer* and *fasting* go in one ear and out the other: "Whoever has ears to hear, let him hear." Prayer and fasting release things from God that normally would not be released.

My biggest concern is not fake news or governmental overreach (though they are a concern); my greatest concern is the apathy of most Christians toward the things of God. When we are full of fleshly appetites, it leaves little room for the Spirit. Those full of pride lack humility. Those full of covetousness lack generosity. Those full of anger lack love, and those always full of food often lack the fullness of the Spirit. Our shopping carts are full of food and drink, but our prayer closets are empty.

When we deal seriously with our sin of apathy, God will deal seriously with us, and our prayers will begin to reflect His will. Then He will take great joy and receive double glory in answering them. We need to be revived because we need spiritual power via prayer in these dire times. I remember when . . .

- the church sought God in an upper room for days until fire fell.
- we were not in a hurry, and extended worship services drove us to our knees.
- we prayed for people, and they were healed.

- people were excited about seeking God rather than making excuses.
- we took authority over the demonic realm.

Never forget that the weakest saint on their knees makes Satan tremble! Prayer is not an insignificant activity; it's an essential. Many sing the famous lyrics, "This is how I fight my battles." But at some point, we have to fight and not just sing. Prayer and fasting are the primary weapons of spiritual warfare.

In dire situations, repentance, fasting (with the right attitude), and prayer are always prescribed. Isaiah 58:1 reminds pastors and authors to "Shout with the voice of a trumpet blast." We must confront spiritual apathy to change it. We must confront sin to spark revival. In the book of Joel, for example, God's blessings were fading, and the people faced enormous devastation. The prophet didn't say sit at home and complain. He said, "Consecrate a fast, call a sacred assembly; gather the elders and all the inhabitants of the land into the house of the LORD your God, and cry out to the Lord" (Joel 1:14 NKJV). When all hope is gone, God is not gone. Cry out to Him!

Joel reminds us that fasting is a priority from the greatest to the least among us. We also see the importance of desperation. The desperate are truly hungry for God. Be encouraged: Moses received the Word of God when he fasted. King Jehoshaphat experienced victory. Esther received protection. Elijah was restored and renewed. Daniel experienced the supernatural. Ezra received direction and safe passage. Nehemiah was strengthened. Joel offered the cure for judgment. Jesus was empowered. And on and on it goes. Many prayers in the Bible were answered when full stomachs were replaced with full hearts. Fasting is spiritual warfare. Even though you might lose a battle, you don't have to lose the entire war. Get up and keep fighting and keep fasting.

When you combine prayer (real prayer, where it becomes a daily priority) with fasting, you gain tremendous spiritual muscle. This is why the enemy hates prayer and fasting. He knows that prayer is a great sin-killer, fear-quencher, power-bringer, victory-giver, holiness-promoter, lust-eliminator, obstacle-remover, time-changer, life-sustainer, demon-slayer, wisdom-giver, peace-elevator, depression-lifter, anxiety-demolisher, anger-suppressor, weakness-remover, strength-booster, and a revival-stimulator. Anything negative is counterbalanced during prayer. When the church prays, it has power. Revival is a gift of love. God cares about the spiritually dead.

The third element that the Lord commanded through Joel the prophet was the gathering together of the people to worship. Prayer and fasting are amplified in the presence of our brothers and sisters kneeling beside us, lifting one another up before the Lord, and crying out for revival with a unified voice. This is what the enemy has been attacking with the pandemic—seeking to prevent God's people from the solemn assembly, from gathering together to cry out to the Lord. Matthew 18 is an oft repeated verse (usually, out of context) but is a powerful reminder of the importance of the gathering together of the saints: "Again I say to you that if two of you agree on earth concerning anything that they ask, it will be done for them by My Father in heaven. For where two or three are gathered together in My name, I am there in the midst of them" (Matthew 18:19–20).

Why do you think Satan is trying to keep you busy and full? Why do you think he is trying to draw you back into sin and addiction? Why do you think he wants you to stay bitter, angry, and critical? To rob you of spiritual power, "to steal and kill and destroy" (John 10:10). We must change that and cry out like the saints of past revivals, "Oh God, rend the heavens and come down!" We must return to the prayer closet and return to hungering and thirsting for God!

Be encouraged because Isaiah 58 offers incredible hope. Although the context supports Israel returning to God, the principles still apply to us today: "Then your light will shine out from the darkness, and the darkness around you will be as bright as noon. The Lord will guide you continually, giving you water when you are dry and restoring your strength. You will be like a well-watered garden, like an ever-flowing spring. Some of you will rebuild the deserted ruins of your cities. Then you will be known as a rebuilder of walls and a restorer of homes" (vv. 10–12 NLT).

Are you ready to restore your home and our nation? It all begins with repentance, prayer, and fasting. The good news is that you can begin today. No matter how far you have fallen, set your sights on God, and He will see you through.

If revival is being withheld from us, it is because . . . we still refuse to face the unchangeable truth that "It is not by might, but by My Spirit."

– Jonathan Goforth

Seeking

Igniting Revival— Dead Bones Come Alive

On the theme of revival, there are often two groups who get offended:

1. those who have never experienced the fire of God and think they don't need it
2. those who don't want to experience God because they are content with comfortable Christianity

In both cases, dead bones must come alive.

The first group is blinded by spiritual pride; a critical heart always quenches the fire of the Spirit. Spiritually proud people don't like to talk about the work of the

Spirit, but they love to argue theology. Like a sinner who doesn't want to talk about sin, many Christians avoid the topic of revival and the deeper work of the Spirit because they are convicted of their spiritual lack.

When challenged about their lack of Holy Spirit fire, these believers often say, "Fire is a sign of judgment. Why would I want that?" While fire can be a sign of judgment for the unbeliever, fire is a mighty filling of the Spirit in a Christian. In Matthew 3:11, John the Baptist tells his disciples that Jesus would baptize believers in the Holy Spirit and with fire. Fire is undesirable in regard to God's judgments, but it's very good in regard to believers receiving the fire of God.

Charles Spurgeon once said, "The fire in the preacher sent of God is not that of mere excitement . . . there is also a mysterious influence resting on God's servants which is irresistible. The Holy Ghost sent down from heaven anoints all true evangelists, and is the true power and fire."[12] I love what Leonard Ravenhill said as well: "The Word does not live unless the unction is upon the preacher. Preacher, with all thy getting, get unction [get fire] or get out of the pulpit."[13]

As a matter of historical fact, genuine revivals all bring the fire of God. The Cambuslang Revival of 1742 often comes to my mind. The website Beautiful Feet records it succinctly:

> The Church of Scotland pastor William
> M'Culloch had a passion for God, and in
> February 1741 he began to preach in his

Cambuslang church about the importance of being born again. M'Culloch was in communication with Jonathan Edwards in America and received news about the revival that was taking place in the American colonies (First Great Awakening). He would read the revival accounts to his congregation and the passion for God increased. . . .

On July 6, 1742, George Whitefield visited Cambuslang and preached 3 times on the day of his arrival, to a vast body of people. His last sermon began at nine in the evening and continued till eleven. The hunger for the Word of God was so strong that the pastor preached after him till past one in the morning. Even then the people could hardly be persuaded to depart. All night, in the fields, the voice of prayer and praise was to be heard.

Whitefield commented about this day: "It far out-did all that I ever saw in America. For about an hour and a half there were scenes of uncontrollable distress, like a field of battle. Many were being carried into the manse [pastor's home] like wounded soldiers [because they were overcome with severe conviction of sin]."[14]

Be clear here: Revival is not about acting weird; it's about the power of God reviving hearts. Whether it's the 1802 revival at Yale University, the 1863 Great Revival in the Confederate Armies, or the famous revival on the

Island of Lewis in 1949 that was recently made popular by "Donald's Bible" on YouTube, all of them centered on reviving dead hearts.[15]

Not surprisingly, the conditions prior to revival are always dark and bleak. God's people often feel hopeless, but this despair can drive us to our knees. According to testimonies of people present at past revivals, the church is often dead, and legalism and spiritual compromise are running rampant—sometimes even to the point where the greatest resistance to the move of God comes from the church! It is at this point of greatest need that God calls a remnant of people to prayer and fasting, and revival is born. In short, revival is often fueled by hungry seekers desperate for more of God.

Beautiful Feet also records the atmosphere leading up to the revival on the Island of Lewis:

> Peggy and Christine Smith prayed in their cottage from 10 p.m. till 3 a.m., while the ministers and others prayed in a barn-like structure and in other locations. . . . After several weeks of praying like that, one evening, while the minister and church leaders (including both men and women) were praying in a barn, a young deacon read from Psalm 24:3-5.
>
> "Who shall ascend into the hill of the Lord? or who shall stand in his holy place? He that hath clean hands, and a pure heart; who hath not lifted up his soul unto vanity, nor sworn deceitfully. He

shall receive the blessing from the Lord, and righteousness from the God of his salvation."

When he closed his Bible he looked at the minister and the others and said, "It seems to me to be so much humbug to be praying as we are praying, to be waiting as we are waiting, if we ourselves are not rightly related to God." He then prayed, "God, are my hands clean? Is my heart pure?"

Immediately, at around 3 a.m., the presence of God gripped every person present. It wasn't only them that sensed this, for the entire village and larger surrounding area sensed that same awareness of God. The following day everyone was absorbed by the reality of eternal things. That group of intercessors left the barn at that early hour and found men and women kneeling along the roads, crying out to God for mercy. Every home had lights on in it, as no one could sleep with the awareness of God being so overwhelming.[16]

These stories are born out of genuine, God-sent revival. Sadly, many reject revival with words similar to these: "Revivals are too emotional. People are just getting carried away." And because of pride, they never experience a powerful move of God's Spirit. But others of us are crying, "Lord, do it again! Shake heaven and awaken my soul. Revive me again so that I can rejoice in you!"

A popular contemporary worship song captures the essence of one pleading with God for His refiner's fire to purify them. The worshiper asks, like Moses, to witness God's glory and for the weight of it to bring him to his knees. Let this be your plea as well.

Is Microwave Christianity Still on the Menu?

The second group who spurns revival is what I call "Las Vegas Christians." They don't want the power of God because they love the power of sin. The lukewarm church hates conviction. They say that they fear God, but they don't live like it. They indulge temptation rather than fight it. They enjoy sin rather than confront it—they have the appearance of glitter and beauty in the dark of night, but the bright light of the sun shows the dirty facade. They mock those who seek holiness and chide those who want to truly live for God. God's Word is clear: The power of the Spirit is always hindered by a sinful lifestyle. The Las Vegas Christian is only concerned with pleasure, ease, and maintaining appearances. They are those who "sat down to eat and drink, and rose up to play" (1 Corinthians 10:7). Sin fascinates before it assassinates!

Whatever group you're in, the only way for dead bones to come alive is to first recognize that you are spiritually dead. Many have a form of microwave Christianity. "People are bored," they say, not realizing that church is boring because the power of God has vanished. Like Samson, they don't know that the Spirit of the Lord has departed (Judges 16:20). But there is hope.

We can once again position ourselves to seek God and his promise that we referenced earlier: "You will seek Me and find Me, when you search for Me with all your heart" (Jeremiah 29:13). "To seek" in this context means to "find what is missing." The Hebrew word for seek, *baqash*, has a very strong meaning. Imagine losing your child in a crowded mall. How would you spend your time? Where would your energy be concentrated? Now parallel this with seeking God.

When you seek something wholeheartedly, it becomes the priority of your life. Whenever God's people drifted in the Old Testament, and when they drift today, it's because they fail to give God preeminence in their lives. Jeremiah and Deuteronomy both offer a wonderful promise: "You will seek me and find me when you seek me with all your heart" (Jeremiah 29:13 NKJV; see also Deuteronomy 4:29). Consider going to bed earlier so you can seek Him earlier the next day. Read encouraging books before you go to sleep rather than watch garbage on the television or other media outlets. What you feed your mind plays a huge role in encouraging you to seek God or discouraging you from it. To ignite personal revival, we must "set our hearts" back to the right position of seeking God, much like a surgeon resets a bone: "Set your heart and soul to seek the LORD your God" (1 Chronicles 22:19 NKJV).

The opposite of *ignite* is to extinguish, suffocate, and quench. What good are an extinguished fire, a suffocated voice, and a dull knife? We must make seeking God a priority since it will never happen on its own. The default position of the flesh is always to drift away from God. We have to fight the daily pull of filth trying to penetrate our lives. As the famous poem by an unknown author goes:

> All the water in the world,
> However hard it tried,
> Could never sink the smallest ship
> Unless it gets inside.
> And all the evil in the world,
> The blackest kind of sin,
> Can never hurt you in the least
> Unless you let it in.

The Power of Prioritizing

As funny as it may sound, we must make plans to seek God. We need to adjust schedules and calendars to put Him first in our lives. Take a quick glance at your calendar and checkbook to see what's really important. But be warned: When we decide to seek God, it's almost as if all hell is unleashed to stop us. The main tool that the enemy uses is busyness—busy with the cares of this life. As a result, God often takes a backseat and stays there for the rest of our lives if we don't fight to pursue Him.

First, commit today to begin removing things that pull you away from God. Granted, emergencies, important meetings, and urgent engagements will happen. I'm not talking about those types of things. I'm talking about making changes to your everyday life. For example, for over two decades I haven't watched much TV, especially at night. At the time of this writing, it's been months since I have watched anything on television. The reason is so I spend that time pursuing God via reading and praying. Every few months, someone says, "I can't believe that you get so much done!" But the key to productivity is available to most of us: Prioritize your life, and remove things that zap your time and steal your energy.

By reading good books or praying before bed, I wake up hungry for more of God instead of hungry for more of the world. Whatever you feed your mind becomes the dominating influence in your life. Granted, don't use me as the standard. I fumble and make mistakes often. I'm simply illustrating the importance of making simple changes that have profound results.

Although this may not apply to everyone, one of the best decisions I ever made was to give up my coffee addiction. Even though it hindered my time with God, I pleaded with Him for years, "Please, can I have just one strong cup?" But God knows what's best. Caffeine is a powerful drug (a stimulant) that affects many of us negatively. It can cause anger and irritability, which aren't good attitudes to have when trying to seek God. I would be so amped-up every morning that I couldn't be still before God. My mind was going one hundred miles an hour. I could relate to an article that reported that researchers at Marshall Space Flight Center documented how various substances, including caffeine, affect spiderweb patterns.[17] It took some hard work and God's grace to eventually break free of this addiction that also brought unhealthy anxiety and irritability.

Secondly, make a prayer list, and go to war when you have the most energy. I have prayers written on a dry erase board as well as index cards. As I pray, I also read the Bible. I'm able to give God the freshest part of my day: the early hours of the morning. During this time, countless sermons have been birthed, and God poured wisdom into my heart. But this is also the time to prepare for spiritual warfare. We do battle on our knees so we can lead on our feet as we contend for our families, nation, and church.

If you're a night person, that's fine too. Whatever the time, give God your best hours, but expect demonic opposition that will try to sidetrack you with busyness. I'm often reminded of Ephesians 6:12 (NKJV), "We do not wrestle against flesh and blood, but against principalities, against powers, against the rulers of the darkness of this age, against spiritual hosts of wickedness in the heavenly places."

When you seek God wholeheartedly, demons cannot defeat you. Haters cannot silence you. People cannot break you. Money cannot buy you. Trials cannot stop you. Fear cannot control you. The devil cannot seduce you. The government cannot overthrow you. And addiction cannot hold you. There's no greater feeling than reaping the benefits of seeking God. As Vince Lombardi said, "I firmly believe that any man's finest hour, the greatest fulfillment of all that he holds dear, is that moment when he has worked his heart out in a good cause and lies exhausted on the field of battle—victorious." If they can say this about football, how much more when we lie victorious on the field of spiritual battle?

Thirdly, to properly seek God with all our heart, we must remove hindrances such as besetting sin. Idolatry shaped in sports, entertainment, success, lust, and the like all damage a seeking heart. I'm assuming the reader understands that I'm not saying one can't enjoy a sporting event or concert now and then. But I'm referring to a lifestyle that puts God on the backburner so other interests can be pursued. David Wilkerson once said, "It is impossible to maintain the joy of the Lord if sin is present in one's life. We must increasingly separate ourselves from the world around us. How can the Holy Spirit pour out joy on a people who continue to indulge in adultery, addictions and materialism, living like those who do not follow Christ?"[18]

Conclusion

Be encouraged; God may sometimes feel far away, but that's the time to press in even more. This pressing strengthens faith, builds spiritual muscle, and deepens our resolve to seek Him with all our hearts. It's been said, "Pray the hardest when it's the hardest to pray." Your feelings are the caboose of the train, not the engine. They shouldn't lead, but they should at least follow. It's easy to seek God when you feel like it, but it's crucial to seek Him even when you don't. This is why faith plays a huge role in pursuing God. Pray, "God, I want the fullness of Your Spirit, and I'm willing to do whatever it takes to experience it." He will honor that prayer if you honor your commitment.

Now that we've looked at the vital importance of humility, prayer, and placing God in the center of our life, the last ingredient found in 2 Chronicles 7:14 is how we view sin. Let's take a quick look at repentance.

In revival, God is not concerned about filling empty churches, He is concerned about filling empty hearts.

– Leonard Ravenhill

Repentance

Desperate for Change

"I will never change! I keep failing. God, please help me," said the once happy person who has been defeated time and again by sin. Change is difficult, but we risk endless difficulties and, often, tragedies if we don't repent and change. Change requires self-examination, grace, responsibility, humility, discipline, obedience, and repentance—character qualities that run countercultural.

We have enough books and sermons on change to fill countless libraries. Yet our problem isn't with "how to," it's with "want to." If you've read my book *Desperate for More of God* or if you've heard me speak to men, you've probably heard the story below as well as most of the points in this section. They seem to strike a chord of conviction, so I include them in this chapter as well.

I vividly remember a men's conference where I spoke on the dangers of pornography. A man approached me after the message, his eyes were filled with tears, and said, "My wife is leaving me because of porn. This conference is my last chance." After talking and praying, we saw that his desire was being fed primarily through a cable-TV sports channel. Many of the explicit commercials and the cheerleaders and photos sparked lust. After a few minutes, I said, "In addition to repentance, accountability, and transparency, remove the television and disconnect the internet for a while. Show your wife that your marriage is worth more." His response was alarming but characteristic of many today: "I can't do that. I'm a sports fanatic."

Surprised and disappointed, I asked, "How badly do you want it? How badly do you want a healthy marriage and a vibrant relationship with the Lord? How badly do you want the abundant life that Christ spoke of? How badly do you want to be a godly role model for your kids? Obviously, not bad enough." I ask the same question today, "How badly do you want it?" It all starts here. You must be *desperate for change.*

Jesus often asked, "Do you want to be made well?" (John 5:6). Although theologians are divided on the motive behind such questioning, one thought is clear: We must "want" to change, not just talk about it. Take anger, for example. It does not produce good fruit (see James

1:20). What about controlling the tongue? The Lord hates gossip, backbiting, and slander. What about wrong attitudes? Self-righteousness and judgmentalism are dangerous. What about addictions? These include anything from foods to drugs to alcohol to pornography and many other unhealthy lusts. Sadly, many do not want to change. In fact, our flesh revels in sin.

The first step toward change is repenting of pride as well as other destructive areas in your life. C. H. Spurgeon rightly noted, "We are never, never so much in danger of being proud as when we think we are humble." When challenging people in this area, I often ask, "Are you genuinely sorry and repentant, or are you just sorry that your reputation and life are on the verge of being ruined?" The difference between sorrow and repentance is vital, and many confuse the two. It's possible to be sorry about the "consequences" but not truly repentant. A penitent person turns from sin—anger, for example, subsides, not remains. They accept full responsibility for their actions without blame, resentment, or bitterness.

When repentance is genuine, we want to be reconciled with those we've injured. We seek forgiveness without conditions and stipulations. We take full responsibility for our actions. There can be no "buts" when repentance is genuine. "I am sorry," "I was wrong," and "Please forgive me" are often healing words and signs of repentance. If this is not occurring, repentance has not taken place. Excuses need to stop before change and restoration can occur.

Christopher Morgan reminds us that "there can be no agreement as to what salvation *is* unless there is agreement as to that from which salvation rescues us. It is impossible to gain a deep grasp of what the cross achieves without plunging into a deep grasp of what sin is."[19] In short, we cannot minimize the damage and destruction of sin. Jesus didn't die on the cross for a "shortcoming" or for a "predisposition"; He died to rescue us from the hellish grip of sin.

Repentance is our only hope and the main catalyst for revival. As Iain H. Murray rightly noted in his incredible work *Revival and Revivalism: The Making and Marring of American Evangelicalism 1750-1858*: "All awakenings begin with the return of a profound conviction of sin. From attitudes of indifference, or of cold religious formality, many are suddenly brought by the hearing of the truth to a concern and distress so strong that it may even be accompanied by temporary physical collapse."[20]

Hearing Is Not Doing

Some have suggested that repentance is just self-improvement or a call to fulfill our natural potential. When we repent, we do improve, and our God-given potential becomes more apparent, but repentance is not about self-improvement—it's about renouncing and turning from sin. Repentance is a change of mind that leads to a change in action. Brokenness, genuine sorrow over sin, and humility are marks of sincere repentance. Lasting hope and joy are also by-products of a right relationship with God, beginning with repentance. There is always a link between genuine change and sincere repentance.

On numerous occasions when I have spoken about the danger of sin from the pulpit or during counseling, most people enthusiastically agree that it's wrong, but they continue anyway. They "hear" but do not "do," and thus, according to James 1:22, they deceive themselves. Pride is deceptive; it blames everyone else but fails to look within. I remember a time when I, along with a few others, confronted a man about his pride. Instead of recognizing his blind spot, he threw it back on those in the room. Unable to perceive his own pride, the man allowed sin's deception to take over, and spiritual blindness set in. When pride gains a stronghold, the heart hardens, and an array of excuses follows. "Sin when it is fully grown brings forth death" (James 1:15 ESV)—death of relationships and death of spiritual health and vitality.

Repentance, followed by obedience, is crucial. This duo stops sin dead in its tracks. The only way out of pride is to do what is right, regardless of feelings. Feelings often deceive, but obedience can be trusted. Sadly, many do not experience freedom and true restoration because wholeness is found in obeying the truth, not just in hearing it. For some people, church serves therapy for this very reason. They hear about sin, are convicted, and leave feeling justified because they "heard" and "felt," but they neither repent nor change. Or the opposite occurs: They never hear about sin, so change through repentance does not occur.

James tells us, "What does it profit, my brethren, if someone says he has faith but does not have works . . . faith by itself, if it does not have works, is dead" (James 2:14, 17). Rather than promote a works-based religion, Scripture demonstrates the importance of having a genuine relationship with Christ for the believer, who, in return, seeks to honor God and others through obedience. Genuine faith is reflected in obedience to God and His Word. The fruit that follows is sincere humility, selfless love, true repentance, and disengagement from the things of the world, instead of self-love. Does your life reflect these characteristics? Both hearing and obeying the truth are equally vital.

As a word of encouragement to those who have failed, if you feel discouraged, don't be! You can get back on track. Often, you'll have two choices—to fall backward or to fall forward. If you choose to fall forward into forgiveness, in time, God's grace will heal and restore you, but it begins with humility . . . humble yourself today, and end the cycle of pride. God can rebuild your life and open doors you might not have thought possible.

Hidden in Plain Sight

Social media is filled with jealousy and envy. Self-indulgence is rampant in the church. Sexual sin has reached an epidemic, and some churches are compromising the gospel in an attempt to reach the culture. Granted, we are called to reach out to others, but not at the expense of compromise. I've witnessed soft-porn images on Christian websites, questionable movie clips during PowerPoint sermons, and youth pastors talking about their favorite sexually charged TV show or movie with the youth, all under the guise of "relating" to the culture. And we wonder why the American church is powerless?

Benson's Commentary is spot on when referencing our theme verse, 2 Chronicles 7:14: "They must humble themselves under his hand, must pray for the removal of the judgment, must seek his face and favour: and yet, all this will not be sufficient, unless they turn from their wicked ways, and return to him from whom they have revolted."[21] And Isaiah 59:1–2 (NIV) reminds us, "Surely the arm of the LORD is not too short to save, nor his ear too dull to hear. But your iniquities have separated you from your God; your sins have hidden his face from you, so that he will not hear."

We run the risk of having "perverted the words of the living God" (Jeremiah 23:36) by failing to warn and challenge people to turn from their sin. Pastors and elders, especially, as the church falls deeper into self-reliance and further from reliance on God, must be bold leaders. Change will only occur when there is a strong conviction of sin, genuine faith, humility, and sincere repentance—may God grant us the wisdom and strength to proclaim these truths. We must stop showing "contempt for the riches of [God's] kindness, forbearance and patience, not realizing that God's kindness is intended to lead [us] to repentance" (Romans 2:4 NIV) and preach with conviction from the pulpits again.

Repentance is our only hope. The key to revival is hidden in plain sight.

Leonard Ravenhill contrasted Hosea with Psalm 86 regarding God's sovereignty and our responsibility in seeking revival. Hosea 10:12 says that if we sow in righteousness we will reap in mercy, but we must break up the fallow ground of our hard hearts and seek God. Breaking up fallow ground is our job, and repentance is the shovel and blade that prepares the soil. Soil cannot receive a downpour until it's plowed. But we also see God's sovereignty in Psalm 85:6: "Will You not revive us again, that Your people may rejoice in You?" It's evident that joy was missing; joy always follows repentance.

In this same vein of thought, Ravenhill also offered a great analogy: "A man who apparently drowned had been under the water for an incredible amount of time. Then somebody pulled him out and worked and worked on him, and eventually life came again. This is actually what it means to be revived . . . it means to revitalize; to restore lost power; to recover lost energy."

If you are spiritually dead to the things of God, don't wait another day. Don't continue to abuse the grace of God. Turn to God today, whether it's for the first time or if you're returning to Him. You are not guaranteed another day. Someone once said to me, "I'll have another shot at God someday." But I never saw that person again. Don't play games. Today is the day of salvation. Turn to Him in full surrender, and embrace what is hidden in plain sight.

If we want revivals, we must revive our reverence for the Word of God.

– Charles Spurgeon

Fasting

Fasting Adds
Spiritual Strength

If I've learned one thing pastoring, it's this: When you allow the Holy Spirit to take control of your physical appetite, your spiritual appetite for God increases.[22] Basil, Bishop of Caesarea (AD 330–379), said, "Fasting begets prophets, strengthens strong men. Fasting makes lawgivers wise; it is the soul's safeguard, the body's trusted comrade, the armour of the champion, the training of the athlete."[23]

Fasting doesn't make God love me more, but I sure love Him more when I choose to fast. Fasting involves prevailing prayer—we go from asking to seeking to knocking. It's been said that fasting meets all the requirements of 2 Chronicles 7:14; it certainly involves humility, prayer, seeking God, and turning from sin.

Fasting also adds spiritual strength to our lives through the discipline it takes. We are encouraged to discipline our bodies because we cannot effectively be filled with the Spirit when we lack discipline. Our faith is not a passive faith but an active one. Romans 6:16 (NASB) explains, "Do you not know that when you present yourselves to someone as slaves for obedience, you are slaves of the one whom you obey, either of sin resulting in death, or of obedience resulting in righteousness?" In other words, you are a slave—you're either God's servant or a slave to your passions and desires. And so through fasting, we are able to bring our fleshly cravings under control.

According to 2 Timothy 1:7, self-discipline is a fruit of the Spirit. Those who say that self-discipline is legalism are dead wrong. We are called to yield to the Spirit and quench sin. But when we yield to sin, we quench the Spirit. Carnal appetites are subdued when fasting, although it is challenging because the flesh always wants to negotiate with us. It says, "Can't we meet in the middle? Don't completely remove food—that's too extreme!"

Self-control is also required for leadership. In Titus 1:8 (NIV), Paul adds that a leader must be "self-controlled, upright, holy and disciplined." John Wesley required fasting of his leaders so they would discipline their appetites rather than allow their appetites to rule them. It's been said for centuries that no man who cannot command himself is fit to command another. Paul told the Corinthian believers, "I discipline my body and bring it into subjection, lest, when I have preached to others, I myself should become disqualified" (1 Corinthians 9:27). An *undisciplined leader* is an oxymoron.

We revisit our passage in Joel to witness the power of fasting: "Consecrate a fast, call a sacred assembly; gather the elders and all the inhabitants of the land into the house of the Lord your God, and cry out to the Lord" (Joel 1:14). The magnitude of the situation determined the response. God's people had departed from Him, and the call was to return through fasting, prayer, and brokenness. Fasting deprives the flesh of its appetite as we pray and seek God's will and mercy. We are saying, "The flesh got me into this predicament. Now it's time to seek God's mercy and humble myself before Him."

Obviously, people have overcome challenges without fasting, but fasting adds extra strength, especially when overcoming addictions. One addiction may end, but others can continue. The alcoholic switches to caffeine, the nicotine addict switches to sugar, and the opioid user switches to food. Fasting can break the never-ending cycle. However, fasting is not a cure-all or a magic wand; it's a spiritual discipline designed to aid in victory.[24]

As the flesh submits through fasting, a stagnant spiritual life turns into "rivers of living water" (John 7:38). The mind becomes uncluttered and focused. The things of God, rather than the things of the world, begin to dominate our thinking. Why wait? Begin today. You've probably fallen so many times that you have lost count— so have I. Don't focus on past mistakes. Get up and try again. God knows our hearts are not perfect, but He looks for humility, brokenness, and dependence on Him. Blessings flow from simple obedience. For example, we had approximately one million sermon views on all our platforms in less than two months, which I believe was a direct result of fasting. I don't say this to elevate anyone, but to show the power of God even in the midst of trials if we look to Him. In short, who can stop God almighty?

The Physical Affects the Spiritual

Can we pray and seek God with all our heart with a headache, tight pants, and a sluggish, lethargic body strung out on our favorite addictive substance? Of course not. Does the way you feel affect your productivity and the quality of your life? Absolutely. Our diet affects key hormones such as serotonin for relaxation, dopamine for pleasure, glutamate for healthy thinking, and noradrenaline for handling stress. If we allow junk food and addictions to control our attitude and productivity, it will hinder what we do for God. When we're always dealing with stress, anxiety, and sickness, can we do much for God? No, we will be limited. Granted, there are those who, through no fault of their own, have a debilitating illness. I'm assuming the reader understands that I'm talking to those who *can* make changes.

What you put in the mouth (body) and the mind (soul) affects the spirit, and when you feed the spirit, it affects the body and the soul. I'm often asked to pray for people with panic attacks, angry outbursts, and anxiety. That can be done, and God honors prayer, but are we opening the door to these things by not halting highly addictive caffeine, sugar, opioid, or nicotine habits? Or are we renewing our minds by meditating on the Word and spending time in prayer? The physical affects the spiritual, and the spiritual affects the physical. Much of the healing I have witnessed over the years was the result of renewed stewardship of the body.

We also know that many emotions, such as anger, bitterness, and jealousy, are toxic to the body. Health also involves healthy emotions. Having a forgiving, loving, joy-filled heart does wonders for the body. Serotonin, for example, is increased when the heart is right. This crucial chemical (also affected by diet and exercise) impacts our mood at a deep level and contributes to an overall state of well-being.

Unless God calls you to fast immediately (and He may), at a minimum, wean yourself off coffee, strong tea, soft drinks, nicotine, sugar, and processed food before fasting—it will aid your success. Prepare yourself by getting your body and mind ready. If possible, wean off everything that is hurting your health, both spiritual and physical. As I said in my book *Feasting and Fasting*, "Most choices lead either to the filling of the Spirit or to quenching and grieving Him." Giving in to one area of weakness lowers our defense in other areas. This aligns with 1 Peter 2:11, in which Peter urges his readers to "abstain from fleshly lusts which wage war against the soul."

My Fasting Journey as I Authored This Book

I chose to fast using primarily water most of the time for two weeks while writing this book. The fast was exhilarating yet challenging. At times, I felt the incredible presence of God. After the first week, for example, as I was preaching, I could sense marvelous strength and spiritual power during the whole message.[25] But at other times, I wondered if God was even listening to my prayers. Sometimes I had tremendous energy, but other times I needed to rest. There was joy unspeakable mixed with irritability and anger. When we fast, our emotions and energy levels are often all over the place. This is to be expected.

There were times I wanted to quit, but I've learned not to make emotional decisions right away. When you begin a fast, write down your goals and prayer requests before you start. My list helped me persevere. When I complete a fast, I feel a release; I have peace. But if I end early, I experience a day or two of regret.

One of my goals was to pray and read more and spend more time with my family. I was seeking better health too. To accomplish this, I had to make minor adjustments such as having two scoops of protein powder if I was feeling extremely weak and needed to preach. One day I even had dinner with my family and enjoyed their fellowship, then returned to water fasting the next day.

Sometimes I would have low-calorie bone broth and a sparkling water drink to get me through the day. Believe it or not, having a little food now and then can actually be harder. The hunger hormone ghrelin is stimulated when a little food or juice is consumed, and one must then fight food cravings again. After three full days of fasting, most people are not that hungry, but getting through those first three days can be the most difficult part of a fast.

Hardcore fasting advocates will chide me for what I just mentioned. Many won't even put lemon juice in their water, but I'm not trying to please others; my goal is to please God. As a type-A perfectionist, I believe that God allows failure to keep me humble. I can imagine my flesh wanting to tell people, "This is twenty-one days of water only. Isn't that impressive?" Just when I start doing really well, God has a way of humbling me.

I've seen so many people quit fasting because they can't follow a plan perfectly. I would rather see them succeed with realistic goals then quit because they fall short of perfection. If you can fast perfectly, great, but don't discourage those who can't. Don't allow fasting to become rigid and mechanical or develop into a system of works or a form of asceticism. And don't beat yourself up if you slip—get back up!

I did my fast right during the COVID-19 pandemic, so I was not able to fast on the beach and relax or stay isolated in a cabin. I had to be practical and strategic while stuck at home. I took my one-year-old on hikes, spent time with my wife and four other kids, led a church, worked on this book and wrote articles, preached sermons, managed our radio network—and on and on it goes. With that said, when you fast, it is best to rest if you can.

Unless God wants me to begin immediately, I try to get my body ready a few weeks prior to fasting by consuming healthy food and weaning off caffeine, sugar, and the like. On the day before my fast, I load up on vitamins, minerals, and amino acids so I have ample reserves.

Direction, Not Perfection

On this theme of perfection, John Piper rightly noted, "It is dangerous to hold up a person or ministry or church as a model of fasting. ... Disillusionment often follows naive admiration. No one is without sin, and all our triumphs are mixed with imperfections."[26] Piper continued, "It is a mistake to think that God's way with one of His children will be His way with all."[27] Fasting is between you and God. It is not a competition.

Most of my fasts have not been perfect. I must have said no a thousand times to food, and I'm not going to let a moment of weakness stop me. God can use moments of weakness to strengthen us during the fast. When I am weak, God's strength sees me through. The apostle Paul experienced a struggle in his life as well and kept asking God to take the challenge away. God allows struggles in us too so that His grace becomes sufficient: "For when I am weak, then I am strong" (2 Corinthians 12:10).

Don't let critical people or a critical spirit stop you; use weakness as a stepping-stone rather than a stumbling block. I know people who lied about the number of days they fasted to impress others. They have received their reward in full (see Matthew 6:16). If anything, I try to downplay my fast rather than promote it for this very reason.

Although it's good to stick to the fast you prepared for, it's okay to adjust when needed. An adjustment (versus quitting) may benefit you greatly, unless God told you otherwise, of course. If weight loss is your goal, then a long fast with enough food to get through can also help. If you're fasting for health reasons, from cancer to arthritis, having just water is best to increase the effects of autophagy, which happens when the body begins to consume its waste and diseased cells for fuel. Think of PAC-MAN consuming all the dots on the screen.

When we eat, especially sugar and carbohydrates, it knocks the body out of autophagy. If it's a very small amount, be encouraged that autophagy will work again fairly soon. Just get back on track. But if you consume a large amount of food, then it may take another day of water fasting to engage autophagy again.

Autophagy usually begins after twenty-four hours of consuming nothing but water after your stored glycogen is depleted. Glycogen is the storage tank for glucose. When the storage tanks in the muscles and liver are depleted, your body switches to autophagy and burns fat as fuel. Many studies also point to severe calorie restriction on certain days to aid detox at the cellular level (e.g., around five to seven hundred calories).[28]

Water fasting also seems to slow aging and disease. This is why you shouldn't give up when you blow it. Granted, I'm not encouraging cheating, but I am encouraging "falling forward" when you make a mistake. Most people I know who fast rarely do it perfectly. Fasting is a spiritual battle. Even though you might lose a battle, you don't have to lose the entire war. Get up and keep fighting . . . keep fasting.

If you are fasting to impress people, it's best to humble yourself, eat a little, and move forward. Get your heart right before proceeding. Jesus's warning about telling others that we are fasting had to deal with a hard heart (see Matthew 6:16–18). In my opinion, it's perfectly fine to tell others about your fast if your heart is right and you're trying to encourage them. After all, how did we know about the fasts in the Bible if people, including Jesus, weren't supposed to tell anyone? Hearing other fasting testimonies is powerful and motivating, but be very selective if you do tell others. Most people will not be supportive.

Again, if God told you what type of fast and for how long, then go for it (don't compromise). For example, if God tells you to stop drinking alcohol or using drugs or to give up sugar and junk food, then do it. Don't use what I said as a way to stay in bondage. I'm assuming the reader understands what I'm trying to convey here. But most people need to simply step out in faith. The Bible isn't a how-to book on fasting. It offers examples and encourages fasting but leaves the details to us and the Holy Spirit. Jesus didn't say how or for how long; He said, "When you fast," not "if you fast" (Matthew 6:16). Of all the fasts I've done, I'd estimate that nine out of ten times I simply had to step out in faith.

We must also use wisdom. For example, those on medication may need to consume a small amount of food with their medication, and those getting very sick during a fast or experiencing low blood sugar may need to drink some juice or eat some food periodically.

No doubt many questions such as these are swirling in your mind right now:

- What about intermittent fasting?
- Can I drink coffee or tea?
- Where should I begin?
- Will I lose muscle?
- Won't I lack vitamins and minerals?

And on and on the questions go. I will again direct you to my book *Feasting and Fasting* for the answers to those questions and many more. The book is available as a download on my website.[29] While there, you may want to check out *HELP! I'm Addicted* as well.

Physical Health Is Important Too

I often wonder how many diseases could be prevented and/or reversed by even partial fasts and eating clean. Shouldn't we be good stewards of our bodies as well as our souls? Multiple sclerosis, for example, is a disease where the immune system slowly consumes the protective sheath that covers the nerves. Can this happen because the body is kept in a toxic state and not allowed to heal?

Parkinson's, another problematic disease, is primarily caused by low dopamine levels. In many cases, dopamine-generating cells have died; even experts do not know why these cells die. Could they have been restored, or new ones created, if the body was allowed time to detox and consume life-giving food? Alzheimer's, a deteriorating disease that destroys memory and causes confusion, is caused when brain cells slowly die and healthy ones are not replicated. As a result, brain tissue has fewer and fewer nerve cells and connections. This leads to the mental and physical symptoms that we see in those who suffer from it.

Could fasting, while one is consuming life-building food at other times, reverse or prevent some of these illnesses? Fasting allows the body to heal, and life-giving food provides many healing properties designed to bring restoration and health to the body. A five-day fast does wonders for the body. The current thought in the fitness world is that we need to go at least five days to really benefit from fasting. Bump it up to ten days, and the health benefits are even more rewarding. Granted, any fast should be medically supervised when possible.

Chiropractor Peter Osborne gave a great talk on *The Fasting Transformation Summit* in May 2020. I included an excerpt below to help you get started with fasting:

> Always start with what the client can tolerate. So especially women, because women can be more prone to having trouble fasting. And it doesn't mean that women can't fast. It just simply means you want to be careful. Some women don't do well with fasting at all at first. And it's because of blood sugar dysregulation. If you're fasting, one of the hormonal responses is that your cortisol goes up when you're fasting.
>
> Cortisol is a hormone that's secreted by your adrenal glands. And it tells your liver to dump sugar into your bloodstream. It's because you're not eating. So there's no blood sugar. So your blood sugar drops. And that cortisol comes out to tell your liver to put sugar in your bloodstream. And some people who are under tremendous stress that already have adrenal fatigue don't do well when they fast. It actually causes an hyper, or an exaggerated, cortisol response, which causes weight gain and bloating. And it can cause more fatigue and more brain fog.
>
> So the first step is if your blood sugar is good and if it's very well managed—so you can have your doctor run tests like hemoglobin A1c and

fasting insulin and blood sugar levels. There are other tests like C-peptide. One of my favorite tests is an intracellular glucose-insulin interaction test that tells us about how well your insulin and your sugar are communicating together. And then there are other types of things that you can do like nutrients that are involved in blood sugar regulation. Like chromium and zinc and B vitamins are important for this. So if all that's dialed in and you've got pretty good blood sugar regulation, then fasting is a great tool. And I start people on a 16:8, a 16-hour fast with eight hours of eating. And this is not a caloric restriction diet. It is just simply a time restriction where we're limiting the time that you eat your meals within an eight-hour frame.

So generally what that means is a very early dinner and a brunch instead of a breakfast. So think of it as if you eat dinner at 6 pm, somewhere in that neighborhood and then you wake up at 6 am in the morning, you've already fasted for 12 hours. So you really only have another four hours to wait until that first meal. So that would come sometime around 10 o'clock if you're eating a really early dinner. So that's a 16:8 strategy. I always start people there because I want to see how well they tolerate fasting. And if they do well with that a couple of days, if we really want to try to expedite the healing process, we can go into a 24-hour fast. And if we really want to expedite the healing process, where the real magic happens is in five days. Three-day fasts can be pretty good because there are a number of different things that happen when you fast 36 hours.

There are a number of different things that happen even more greatly when you fast 72 hours. And then when you get into the five-day parameter, what we see is massive, what's called autophagy, which is your cell debris, your broken cells, your old cells are rapidly being removed and being replaced. You can actually see in a good five-day fast a complete replenishment of the immune cells. And that's very important with autoimmune disease because if you've got all these circulating immune cells that are hyperactive and hyper responsive, we want to clear those out of the circulation. But again, the problem with many people who are chronically ill is they can't yet tolerate a five-day fast. So start with a 16:8. Before you do that, make sure that your blood sugar is being well regulated through a fast and has the potential to survive that fast without just creating more of a hormone imbalance and problem with you. And if you tolerate 16:8, try a 24. And if you tolerate a 24, you can 48 or three days. And then expand that out if you would like to.

Again, it's a voluntary thing because not everybody is capable of wrapping their mind around wanting to go five days without food. But it can be very liberating. But it also, in my opinion, should be monitored and should be done strategically because if you go too long and you're trying to do too much, you can get yourself in trouble. So again, if you want the ultimate fast, five days is where the actual magic happens in terms of resetting the immune system in autoimmune disease. But if you're going to attempt that, do it under medical supervision. And make sure that your blood sugar levels are where they need to be and that you're capable of maintaining normal blood sugar without a hyper cortisol excretion.[30]

Conclusion

I pray that this chapter has clarified the role that fasting plays in our spiritual lives. Like prayer and the meeting of the assembly, these spiritual disciplines have largely been neglected in our churches, to the detriment of our spiritual power and our influence in our society. If we are to have any hope of restoring our nation, we must restore the spiritual vitality of our churches, and for that to happen, we must first restore these disciplines in our homes. This requires first a refocus on personal holiness and our own walk with the Lord. In the end, our faith is a personal one, and our hope is in a personal relationship with the Lord that will lead to better relationships with others, and soon our whole society is impacted for the kingdom of Christ.

Post-Pandemic Pastors and the Sin of Silence

Before we conclude, we need to address another hindrance.[31] First, let me state upfront that countless pastors and Christian leaders are currently doing amazing things. Many of them have invested into my life, and I praise God daily for them. But I also see a disturbing trend taking place.

Over the last few decades, Americans have witnessed the destruction of the institution of marriage between a man and a woman, the removal of God's Word in most of the public arena, horrific racism, and the blatant murdering of millions of babies. This is an indictment against America, and the pulpit is partially responsible—

our silence speaks volumes. The pulpit regulates the spiritual condition of God's people, which affects the nation. A lukewarm, sex-saturated culture (and church) simply reflects the lack of conviction in the pulpit as well as the pew.

Pastor Jim Garlow, in a conversation we recently had, rightly noted, "There are approximately 364,000 churches in America; 72 percent, or 264,000 of them, are liberal, meaning that they really don't care about the Bible. According to exhaustive surveys, somewhere between 6,000 and 15,000 actually have a bona fide biblical worldview, that is, they see life through the lens of Scripture."[32] Nearly 72 percent of churches don't look to the Bible as their final source of authority and direction. No wonder America is crumbling from within; the foundation is deteriorating.

He went on to say, "Bold pastors are nearly extinct. It would be much easier 'to play church' and make everyone feel good. The church—as we now know it—will be functionally illegal very soon. With the recent SCOTUS decisions, the First Amendment died, and churches will very soon be forced to hire those who practice homosexuality and will not be allowed to speak against the sinful practice."

This chapter is not a rebuke, per se, but a tear-stained plea to return to God. The blood of unborn children and the effects of ungodly legislation are *not* just on the hands of legislators or judges but also on the hands of capitulating preachers. Society can ignore the murder of millions of babies in the womb, mock the police, desecrate society, pillage and destroy, redefine marriage, support perversion, back ungodly movements, and pastors are supposed to keep their mouths shut on these issues? I don't think so.[33]

The Irony of Silent Watchmen

The Bible calls pastors "watchmen" who cry out and sound the alarm to awaken a sleeping church, not sing it lullabies. The prophet Isaiah doesn't mince words about lazy watchmen. He says they are blind, ignorant, and dumb dogs who cannot bark (raise their voices to warn). They sleep and lie down, loving to slumber (see Isaiah 56:10).

At first glance, you may think this wording is too strong, but backing away from speaking the truth in love is a serious offense against God. A genuine pastor doesn't call himself to the ministry; God calls him to speak the truth, even on tough topics. Silence about sin is rebelling against the call of God. If his sermons do not upset the world from time to time, I have to seriously question his calling.

Few Spirit-filled preachers are left, and when one rises, they are quickly labeled as right-wing, extreme, or narrow-minded. The so-called evangelical church is on the verge of totally capitulating, especially on the cusp of the Supreme Court's recent decisions. These "woke" Christians are not woke to the things of God. They often do more harm than good by hashtagging and promoting false narratives.

Yes, we need to unite against racism and call it out when warranted, but our capitulation has led to cowardliness. In trying to correct the sin of racism, the pendulum has now swung in a dangerous direction. There is only one fix to racism: the gospel of Jesus Christ. Pastors must preach about sin, repentance, and forgiveness; a person can only truly change by turning to Christ. The irony is that many pastors avoid talking about foundational truths of the Bible that lead to real heart change. They are actually part of the problem, not the solution.

Yet didn't God instruct pastors and elders clearly in His Word on what their role was to be? Paul directed Timothy to plainly preach the Word of God:

> I charge you therefore before God and the Lord Jesus Christ, who will judge the living and the dead at His appearing and His kingdom: Preach the word! Be ready in season and out of season. Convince, rebuke, exhort, with all longsuffering and teaching.
>
> – 2 Timothy 4:1–2

And in Paul's letter to Titus, whom he had left in Crete to "set in order the things that [were] lacking, and appoint elders" (Titus 1:5), he instructs Titus to "speak the things which are proper for sound doctrine" (Titus 2:1). He follows this charge with a practical list of what those things are for holiness for older men and women, younger men and women, and bondservants (employees, we might say today). The reason, Paul states, is so "the word of God may not be blasphemed" (v. 5).

In fact, our example was set by the apostles in the time of the newly born church. When there arose a complaint that the Greek widows were being neglected, the apostles handled it rightly by instructing the believers to select seven deacons, for, they said, "it is not desirable that we should leave the word of God and serve tables, . . . but we will give ourselves continually to prayer and to the ministry of the word" (Acts 6:2, 4). What happened as a result? "The word of God spread, and the number of the disciples multiplied greatly in Jerusalem, and a great many of the priests were obedient to the faith" (v. 7). When pastors and elders are obedient to their callings, God blesses—and heals—the church.

The Sin of Prayerlessness

At the heart of cowardliness are the sins of prayerlessness and pride, which are running rampant in many of our churches. The dry, dead, lethargic condition of the church accurately reflects an impotent prayer life and a lack of humility. Yet in Acts 6, the apostles named *two* things to which they would devote themselves: preaching the Word *and prayer.* Prayerlessness in the pulpit leads to apostasy and dead sermons. Prayerlessness in the pew leads to shattered lives and depression. Prayerlessness in men leads to the breakdown of the family. Prayerlessness in Washington leads to the breakdown of society. "When faith ceases to pray, it ceases to live" (E. M. Bounds). We have plenty of demands for protests, but where are the cries for prayer meetings?

When a pastor stands firm for truth, he is demeaned, mocked, and scorned—or people simply leave that church in search of a more "loving" pastor. But this persecution, according to Scripture, can be a badge of honor, as long as our boldness is a fruit of the Spirit and not the fruit of an arrogant heart: "Blessed are those who are persecuted for righteousness' sake" (Matthew 5:10).

Ironically, the closer I draw to Christ through prayer and worship, the bolder I become. But the more I'm concerned with the opinions of others, the more fearful I become. Boldness cannot be worked up; it must be brought down as we surrender our hearts and lives to Jesus Christ. Too many pastors join the ministry not to battle the darkness but to sign a truce with the world.

Pulpits Aflame with Righteousness

A quote often attributed to Alexis de Tocqueville, a Frenchman who authored *Democracy in America* in the early 1800s, helps to identify how far we have drifted: "It was not until I went to the churches of America and heard her pulpits aflame with righteousness did I understand the secret of her success. America is great because she is good, and if America ceases to be good, America will cease to be great." Pastors are not just cheerleaders; they are game-changers. They are called to stir and to convict so that change takes place. Granted, there are many wonderful pastors and churches. I appreciate their ministry, but as a whole, the church has drifted off course. Many have lost the compass of truth. But there is hope if we look in the right direction: "Therefore say to them, Thus declares the Lord of hosts: Return to me, says the Lord of hosts, and I will return to you" (Zechariah 1:3).

That's a life-changing promise for pastors: return to Him, and He will return to you. Boldness comes directly from the Holy Spirit, and it is crystal clear that many of us are not spending a lot of time with God. Everything that God calls pastors to be is compromised when we are too busy and make no time for Him. Many of the activities at church, for example, are good and have their place. But when programs and goings-on in the ministry get in the way of a pastor's true calling, we need to rethink our priorities, possibly even shutting those things down for a time.

A Passionate Plea to Pastors

True preaching comes when the wellspring of what God has deposited into your life is deposited into the hearts of others. But you can't give what you don't have. Dead pastors have dead churches, and cowardly pastors have passive churches. George Whitefield, who many say sparked the First Great Awakening, wrote this in his journal while on a preaching tour of the American colonies: "I am persuaded, the generality of preachers talk of an unknown and unfelt Christ. The reason why congregations have been so dead is because they have had dead men preaching to them."[34]

God doesn't need church buildings, marketing, hype, or promotion; He needs men filled with the Spirit of God. Micah 3:8 declares, "But truly I am full of power by the Spirit of the LORD, and of justice and might, to declare to Jacob his transgression, and to Israel his sin."

I pose a challenge to America's pulpits: Where are the Isaiahs and Jeremiahs calling nations to repentance? Where are the Peters and Pauls who will speak with such authority that martyrdom cannot silence them? Where are the Wycliffes who stand unyielding for the truth? Where are the Tyndales and the Husses, willing to be burned at the stake for declaring the truth? Where are the Luthers, refusing to back down from their faith and exclaim, "Here I stand; I can do no other"?

Where are the John Calvins who are shaping the religious thoughts of our Western culture? Where are the John Knoxes who cry, "Give me Scotland [for the cause of Christ] or I die"? Where are the Whitefields who are shaking continents? Where are the modern-day Howell Harrises, Daniel Rowlandses, and Griffith Joneses who are preaching with passion and ushering in revival?

I ask again, "Where are they?" Where are the John Wesleys, saying, "Give me one hundred preachers who fear nothing but sin and desire nothing but God, and we will shake the gates of hell?" Where are the David Brainerds who are spending so much time in prayer that it convicts the rest of us? Where are the Robert Murray

McCheynes, causing people to weep before even preaching a word?

Where are the Spurgeons, speaking and preaching with such authority as to move queens and nobility? Where are the D.L. Moodys who are bringing America to its knees? Where are the Evan Robertses who preach so powerfully against sin that the people cry out, "No more, Lord Jesus, or I'll die"? Where are the Puritans like Richard Baxter, who say with humility, "I speak as a dying man to dying men"?

Where are men with uncompromising power and authority in the pulpits today? The one thing that all these great men had is the one thing that many today are lacking: authority and the power of the Holy Spirit. They were men of extraordinary prayer, brokenness, and humility, men filled and clothed with power from on high. The men who do the most for God are always men of prayer. Calvin Miller wisely said, "Preaching, in one sense, merely discharges the firearm that God has loaded in the silent place." And Martyn Lloyd-Jones stated, "Preaching is theology coming through a man who is on fire."[35] Are you on fire for God? To affect the pew, it must begin in the pulpit.

Conclusion

The world is on fire. You may not accept that, but it is the truth. This may be God's last warning to America. Can it be saved? I am not sure. When the pulpit is silent, all hell breaks loose because there is no confrontation or conviction of sin. But we are called to fight with the spiritual weapons of prayer and worship, to stand strong, and to expose the unfruitful works of darkness. I will do that until God calls me home. How about you?[36]

Let it not be said of us today, "And there arose another generation after them who did not know the Lord," just because pastors failed to be bold preachers of righteousness. The burden of responsibility rests squarely on our shoulders. It's our choice—stand or fall!

Appendix 1

Answered Prayers Motivate

Over the last two decades, I watched my mom meet once a week with two close friends to pray for family members and our nation. This has been very inspiring for me, and I know that thousands of prayers have been heard. I'd like to share just a few answered prayers with you from when I began my journey back to God.

In 2000, much prayer went into leaving my corporate position with a large fitness center chain, which included giving up all my income and stepping into the unknown. Prayer led to peace and assurance that God had my back. I also knew that I had to move back home to save money, but because that was too embarrassing, I rented an apartment. After losing over five thousand dollars in rent, I finally moved back home. It's always best to listen to God sooner rather than later.

During that same time, I was also spending a lot of time praying for a spouse. As I was praying, I believe that God was telling me, "Instead of finding Miss Right, focus on being Mr. Right." In time, God brought me the perfect helpmeet. No wonder the devil set out to destroy the relationship right off the bat. But prayer held us together.

A few years later, my wife quit her job to have kids. This step was bathed in prayer because, on paper, we could not afford it. Peace and assurance filled our hearts as we stepped out in faith. Soon after, with the help of my brother, I started a construction company, running heavy equipment and working forty-plus hours a week. Suffice it to say, God more than provided.

During that time, we also prayed about buying our first home. Unfortunately, home prices seemed to double between the late 1990s and when we bought our home in 2005. I will never forget the day we went to look at new homes. The pads were already cut for the homes that were to be built soon, and we had to put a deposit down before the phase sold out. I thanked the sales representative and said I need to wait a week or so. She responded, "Okay, but this house won't be here if you wait." But I wasn't about to rush ahead without waiting on God. After a week of praying, we had tremendous peace to put a deposit down.

I will never forget the day we stopped by the sales office to begin the process. As soon as we walked in, the sales rep said, "I'm so sorry. That house is gone. That phase sold out last week, and now the next phase is beginning, but the same model you want is twenty-five thousand dollars more." Yes, that's how fast the market was increasing. It was unbelievable to watch, and it eventually led to the big housing crash around 2008.

When she told us the news, ironically, we still had incredible peace. Within a minute or two, the sales rep turned and said, "Oh, by the way, we just had a house in the older phase fall out of escrow. It's twenty-five thousand dollars cheaper than the one you were going to purchase, it has an extra bedroom, and it's larger." We jumped on it, and the rest is history. We were able to move right in, which was an answer to another prayer we had been praying—to find something move-in ready.

God knows how to bless His children if we wait on Him. In fact, He opened a similar door when we purchased our next home in 2013. We moved in with similar equity. Having a background in real estate, I know that this is nearly impossible, but with God, all things are possible. Granted, I'm not saying that prosperity is always a sign of blessing, but there can be seasons of blessing if we pray and wait on Him.

In 2009, on nothing but a wing and a prayer, we were able to air sermons in San Fernando Valley for fifty dollars each Saturday. The church hadn't launched yet, but God launched the ministry. His favor was evident. January 3, 2010, was a pivotal turning point for us. I was awakened by a prompting saying, "Get up. Let me show you something." When I awoke, no one was there, but I knew that I needed to get right into God's Word for direction. As I read, I received so much confirmation about my calling that we were able to move forward and plant Westside Christian Fellowship on September 25, 2010.

In 2013 I was having a hard time writing my next book. I prayed for weeks, "God, I need motivation." The following week, a large publisher called and wanted to publish my next book. I was puzzled because I always felt that God wanted me to do my books in-house so that we can offer free downloads and reduced prices and give away copies now and then. Nevertheless, I worked frantically, sometimes ten hours a day, on *Desperate for More of God*. After a few months, I sent the rough draft to the publisher, but they turned it down. They wanted a softer message, but that's not my style. So we moved forward, publishing it ourselves. My prayer for motivation was answered.

On May 23, 2015, we joyfully witnessed two of our kids repent and another turn completely to God that same year after questioning their faith. In all those cases, we took it to God every day in focused prayer. Granted, our kids will be a point of prayer until the day we take our last breath, but it's incredible to witness the hand of God when you set out to pray and fast.

In 2016, after not having a building for nearly six years, we were given a wonderful church campus in the rolling hills of Leona Valley. And a few years later, in 2019, we launched the WCF Radio Network. The story of how this came about was exciting to watch. The hand of

God was clearly guiding and leading every step of the way. Although I considered it a crazy idea, especially because the radio stations weren't available at that time, I began to pray. I was reminded that God ultimately has the final say in everything.[37]

And on and on the prayer list goes, from small prayers to large requests. Some prayers we are still waiting on, but one thing is certain: Those who wait on the Lord will see answered prayers and renew their strength.

Encouraging Quotes

The following motivational quotes are from Gordon Cove's book *Revival Now Through Prayer and Fasting*:[38]

It [fasting] is not a good thing to be lightly entered upon, for undoubtedly it will bring you into one of the greatest spiritual battles you have ever fought with satan. Satan does not want you to do it, because he knows that it will lead you on to greater spiritual heights and victories in the Christian life than you have ever reached before.

Fasting is not to weaken the body, but to strengthen the Spirit.

Fasting means that you got to the place of spiritual desperation. It means that you are now determined at all costs to put God first.

But many people excuse themselves by saying that they are not strong enough . . . when all the time they are not really prepared to get desperate with God.

When a person wants a thing so much that he is willing to go without food to obtain that thing, then the fast itself becomes a prayer. It is an inward, outspoken heart cry.

You have not sought the Lord with your whole heart until you have tried a protracted season of prayer and fasting. Many Christians have been praying for years about certain problems. Sometimes these prayers are not answered. But in many cases, where fasting has been added to prayers, along with deep consecration and weeping before God, the answer has miraculously come to hand.

Recommended Reading

Fasting for A Miracle, Elmer L. Towns

Fasting and Eating for Health, Joel Furhman

God's Chosen Fast. Arthur Wallis, CLC Publications

The Beginners Guide to Fasting, Elmer L. Towns

The Ministry of Fasting, J. G Morrison

Fasting (Expanded Edition), Gordon Cove

Fasting Can Save Your Life, Herbert M. Shelton

The Power of Prayer and Fasting, Ronnie W. Floyd

A Hunger for God, John Piper

Revival Now Through Prayer and Fasting, Gordon Cove

Notes

[1] You can also listen to the sermon "The Destabilization of America" at our website at Westside Christian Fellowship at https://westsidechristianfellowship.org/audio/6-14-20-the-destabilization-of-america or watch on YouTube: https://youtu.be/CZhF3DRDZVQ.

[2] Polizette Staff, "CNN sticks to liberal script, ignores black police officers killed in riots," LifeZette, June 8, 2020, https://www.lifezette.com/2020/06/cnn-sticks-to-liberal-script-ignores-black-police-officers-killed-in-riots.

[3] Tony Perkins, "Like a Tweet, Lose a Lease," Family Research Council, June 10, 2020, https://www.frc.org/updatearticle/20200610/tweet-lease.

[4] David Barton, "The Founding Fathers and Slavery," Patriot Press, accessed June 16, 2020, https://www.patriotacademy.com/founding-fathers-slavery.

[5] Listen to more at "The Destabilization of America," YouTube, June 15, 2020, https://youtu.be/CZhF3DRDZVQ.

[6] All three messages can be heard at https://westsidechristianfellowship.org/videos/the-revival-series.

[7] Leonard Ravenhill, *Revival Praying*, Kindle edition, location 924 of 1633.

[8] Iain H. Murray, *Revival and Revivalism: The Making and Marring of American Evangelicalism 1750-1858* (Edinburgh: Banner of Truth, 1994), 163–64.

[9] Duncan Campbell, *The Price and Power of Revival*, accessed June 17, 2020, http://www.thechurchofwells.com/uploads/5/9/9/1/5991751/campbell_d_price_and_power_of_revival.pdf. Duncan Campbell wrote this book many years ago, and it has been reprinted by many different publishers.

More about this incredible man of God and the revivals that he participated in can be found at http://www.sermonindex.net/modules/articles/index. php?view=article&aid=20552.

[10] Campbell, *The Price and Power of Revival*.

[11] Wilbur E. Rees, *$3.00 Worth of God* (Valley Forge, PA: Judson, 1971), 5.

[12] Charles H. Spurgeon, The Complete Works of C. H. Spurgeon, ed. Anthony Uyl (Ontario: Devoted, 2017), 15:52.

[13] Leonard Ravenhill, "Unction!" *Measure of Gold Revival Ministries*, accessed June 17, 2020, http://www.evanwiggs.com/revival/fireham/unction.html. Some have commented that they heard him add "or get out of the pulpit" many times.

[14] Chet and Phyllis Swearingen, "Cambuslang Revival of 1742," Beautiful Feet, accessed June 17, 2020, https://romans1015.com/cambuslang. Many more revival accounts can be found at Beautiful Feet. I encourage you to read them to spark revival hunger in your own heart at https://romans1015.com/accounts-of-revival.

[15] "Donald's Bible," YouTube, April 24, 2020, https://youtu.be/c9qVN50TpCM.

[16] Chet and Phyllis Swearingen, "Revival on the Island of Lewis: 1949-1952," Beautiful Feet, accessed June 17, 2020, https://romans1015.com/lewis-revival.

[17] Alexandra Ma, "An old NASA study gave spiders drugs to see how it affected their webs," *Business Insider*, June 14, 2019, https://www.businessinsider.com/how-powerful-is-caffeine-nasa-spider-web-study-2019-5?fbclid=IwAR1gjaIrlm-5fbn4B_0jPJPbVGlpeJCvipQFbwmJVQj3TiIwhZlWsnXOZUA. See more about coffee in my book *HELP! I'm Addicted*.

[18] David Wilkerson, "Joy Through Repentance," World Challenge, April 30, 2020, https://worldchallenge.org/lv/node/33465.

[19] Christopher Morgan, *Fallen: A Theology of Sin* (Wheaton, IL: Crossway, 2013), 22.

[20] Murray, *Revival and Revivalism*, 163.

[21] *Joseph Benson's Commentary of the Old and New Testaments* (2 Chronicles 7), StudyLight.org, accessed June 23, 2020, https://www.studylight.org/commentaries/rbc/2-chronicles-7.html.

[22] This chapter was written based on personal experience and observation as well as many outside reputable resources. If professional assistance is needed, the services of a capable authority are recommended. The views expressed here should not replace professional medical advice. Readers should seek medical supervision before starting or altering a dietary plan, including fasting.

[23] Quoted in Romara Dean Chatham, *Fasting: A Biblical Historical Study* (Alachua, FL.: Bridge Logos, 2001), 67.

[24] The majority of this section was excerpted from my book *Feasting and Fasting*.

[25] Listen to the sermon "To Be Heard on High," April 26, 2020, YouTube, https://www.youtube.com/watch?v=S5tPxR7-8LA&t=677s.

[26] John Piper, *A Hunger for God* (Wheaton, IL: Crossway, 1997), 93.

[27] Piper, *Hunger for God*, 95.

[28] A good explanation of the process can be found at Paige Jarreau, PhD, "The 5 Stages of Intermittent Fasting" LifeApps, May 18, 2020, https://lifeapps.io/fasting/the-5-stages-of-intermittent-fasting.

[29] Links to my books are available at https://shaneidleman.com/books.

[30] Peter Osborne, DC, DACBN, PScD, "Fasting and Inflammation," Fasting Transformation Summit, May 20, 2020, https://fastingtransformation.com/expert/peter-osborne. Although a five day fast is beneficial, many other benefits follow longer fasts.

[31] This chapter is adapted from Shade Idleman, "Post-Pandemic Pastors and the Sin of Silence," June 20, 2020, ShaneIdleman.com, https://shaneidleman.com/2020/06/20/post-pandemic-pastors-and-the-sin-of-silence.

[32] See "Conversations on Race and the Church: A Call to Action, Part 1," Barna, June 23, 2020, https://www.barna.com/research/a-call-to-action-part-1.

[33] For more on that, I invite you to watch this short clip picked up by Fox News: "Let Me Get This Straight," YouTube, April 8, 2018, https://youtu.be/F-wrToS5YpM.

[34] George Whitefield, *George Whitefield's Journals* (Edinburgh: Banner of Truth Trust, 1998), 470.

[35] D. Martyn Lloyd-Jones, *Preaching and Preachers* (Grand Rapids, MI: Zondervan, 2012), Kindle Edition, 110-111.

[36] For a quick clip on why we can talk about political hot buttons, see "Pastor Shane Discusses Why He Talks About Politics - A Must-Hear for All Americans," YouTube, June 16, 2020, https://youtu.be/czHQticSX_g.

[37] Read the story at "About WCF Radio" at https://wcfradio.org/wcf-radio.

[38] Gordon Cove, *Revival Now Through Prayer and Fasting* (Nicholasville, KY: Schmul, 1988).

Made in the USA
Middletown, DE
28 July 2021